WANDERER'S TAROT
GUIDEBOOK

CASEY ZABALA

WEISER BOOKS

This edition first published in 2023 by Weiser Books, an imprint of
Red Wheel/Weiser, LLC

With offices at:
65 Parker Street, Suite 7
Newburyport, MA 01950
www.redwheelweiser.com

Previously published in 2016 by Casey Zabala.

ISBN: 978-1-57863-819-2

Names: Zabala, Casey, 1990- author.
Title: Wanderer's tarot guidebook / Casey Zabala.
Description: Newburyport, MA : Weiser Books, 2023. | Summary: "This
  companion guide for the Wanderer's Tarot deck has in-depth
  interpretations for each card, including reversals; suggestions for card
  spreads; and a brief history of the tarot"-- Provided by publisher.
Identifiers: LCCN 2023018673 | ISBN 9781578638192 (trade paperback) | ISBN
  9781633413184 (ebook)
Subjects: LCSH: Tarot. | BISAC: BODY, MIND & SPIRIT / Divination / Tarot |
  BODY, MIND & SPIRIT / Goddess Worship
Classification: LCC BF1879.T2 Z33 2023 | DDC 133.3/2424--dc23/eng/20230707
LC record available at https://lccn.loc.gov/2023018673

Cover design by Sky Peck Design
Interior images by Casey Zabala
Interior typeset by Brittany Craig
Typeset in Aller Light
Printed in the United States of America
IBI
10 9 8 7 6 5 4 3 2 1

WANDERER'S TAROT

GUIDEBOOK

To the Goddexx,
in all of their manifestations

Witches cast spells, not to do evil, but to promote changes of consciousness. Witches cast spells as acts of redefinition. To respell the world means to redefine the root of our being. It means to redefine us and therefore change us by returning us to our original consciousness of magical—evolutionary processes. This consciousness is within us, in our biology and in our dreams. It works on subliminal levels, whether or not we are aware of it, because it is the energy of life and imagination. When we are aware of it, it works for us, as the energy of destiny. And it is powerful, with the genuine power of biological life and cosmic imagination.

—Monica Sjöö

Contents

PREFACE

May you divine your path with a fearless sense of adventure and clarity. Seek truth, your truth, while being ever open to changing winds. The time is ever present for knowing thyself—for you are the True North, South, East, and West that will guide you.

Turn to these cards for deeper questioning. Lead yourself through this journey with many allies. These allies should push you to continue when you have lost your way, to warn you of dangerous actions or thoughts, and to remind you of your true beauty. *The Wanderer's Tarot* is an obliging ally, if you are open to the mystery.

The Wanderer's Tarot deck was born of many dreams, divinings, and interactions with the magical tarot pack. She blossomed from a window of inspiration and incubation. The deck was given life through traditional symbolism and iconography. Following patterns of geometry and numerology has allowed the deck to take on a minimalist style, allowing for a spaciousness in the reader's interpretation.

The cards are based on traditional tarot symbolism, and transmuted by the need for feminine insight and awakening. This feminine insight is rooted in receptivity, the wisdom of the darkness, and the desire for healing outcomes for all. For the natural magical practitioner, these cards resonate with our magical tools and talismans. The suits of Moons, Stones, Knives, and Feathers will lead you to a deeper understanding of your personal power—emotionally, materially, mentally, and passionately.

INTRODUCTION

The first time I was introduced to the oracle, I was twelve years old and one of my mother's friends gifted me a mysterious deck of cards. The sun was falling behind the trees, creating a tangled August light. We sat by the river, my mother, her friend, and I, watching the gnats' frenzy above the rivulets of cool, dark matter, softly whispering. I unwrapped the package and was shocked by what I had been given. A deck of cards, speckled with stars and vibrant, illuminating images. We all had our cards read that evening, in the waning summer light, and I still remember what those cards shared with us. After that evening my life was permanently altered. Something about how the cards felt as I shuffled them, and how they could speak with such clarity and grace, enamored me, and I initiated my divinatory practice then and there.

The experience of communicating with a divine source fundamentally changed the way I make meaning in this world. The floodgates had been opened into a new sense of reality. No longer did I feel alienated and alone in a world that had no inherent meaning, empty beauty. Tarot forged a connection to the sacredness in my own existence, to the life force in the seemingly inanimate, and the potential to follow a path that might lead to some grain of truth. The fluidity of my first encounter with divination compounded my understanding that tarot cards offer revelation, particularly for those who have a basic trust in their intuition. I learned that over time, tarot can become a potent ally in honoring and empowering our innate intuitive abilities. Beyond this powerful potential, tarot holds keys for unlocking an understanding of the esoteric undercurrents of humanity. The energies I continue to encounter within the tarot, and the truths it connects us with, are of an esoteric lineage, one that is important to encounter and honor for its full complexity.

The mystical teachings of the tarot are products of a complex network of occult philosophies. In order to fully grasp tarot's teachings, as well as its spiritual capacity, the earnest seeker must endeavor to understand the occult basics. While there is no definitive origin for tarot, there is a rich narrative of occult philosophies that participated in its inception and consequential development throughout the ages. Countless secret societies, mystical orders, and high magicians have shaped and protected the magical art of the tarot, each leaving their mark on the tradition of decks, correspondences, and spiritual energies composing the seventy-eight-card pack. Without a basic understanding of what these cultural currents and thinkers believed and practiced, we will understand very little about the spiritual essence of our beloved tarot packs.

Historical records suggest that the earliest card decks were encoded with tarot symbolism. To understand tarot's spiritual essence, one must examine the culture in which it was formulated. The first *tarocchi* cards were crafted in Italy, in the fourteenth century. These decks were commissioned by wealthy aristocratic families. These ornate decks can be likened to devotional images, and were perhaps used not solely as a deck of cards, or for divination purposes, but for meditation, prayer, and magic. Unlike today, fourteenth- and fifteenth-century Italy was steeped in magical traditions. During that time, hermeticism experienced a resurgence, largely due to the translation of the Corpus Hermeticum by Marsilio Ficino, commissioned by Cosimo de' Medici, a prominent figure in the Italian Renaissance. Astrology was still a respected science, and the use of images to capture and enhance magical essences was widely practiced. Tarot cards emerged during this time, when a magical worldview persisted, and when image and symbol held a powerful grip over the human psyche and interfaced meaningfully with the natural world.

If we accept the basic magical worldview of the Renaissance, we can see how tarot was born within a lineage of image-magic. This means that each archetype and card has the potential to house spirits. For example, the Strength card, with its gentle yet formidable lion tamer, not only represents the power of the will when married with spirit; it actually can invoke the daemon, who enchants wild beasts and embodies effortless grace. Tarot empowers our intuitive faculties; but it also weaves us back into a web of spirit communion and connection. When communing with spirits of any sort, it is wise to have a clear understanding of their character, intentions, and story. To work with the spirits of the tarot, we have to gain a clearer understanding of the lineage of these spiritual identities, hermeticism.

To work with the tarot is to enter into conversation with the hermetic arts, whether one is aware of it or not. Hermeticism was born and blossomed within a cosmological framework that believed all elements of life held inherent meaning. The movements of the sun, moon, and stars dictated harvesting practices, changing seasons, and auspicious periods of time to act or reflect. The ancient Egyptian figure Hermes Trismegistus, believed to be a combination of the Egyptian god Thoth and the Greek god Hermes, famously said, "as above, so below." That is, the macrocosm mirrors the microcosm; all levels of reality are intricately related and correspond to one another. Richard Roberts, a Jungian analyst and tarot reader, frames it from a psychological viewpoint: "as within, so without." This is another way to interpret tarot's symbolism. Each tarot symbol is a mirror through which deeper understanding of oneself can be gleaned. Similarly, through the study of nature, humankind studies the psyche.

Occult symbolism is an amalgamation of many different traditions: numerology, cabalistic cosmology, alchemy, tantra, astrology, the teachings of Pythagoras, the mystery schools of Ancient Greece, hermeticism. And at the heart of the many complex pathways of occult philosophies there is an invitation to live in an enchanted world, one that speaks, listens, and participates in our life paths. When working consciously with tarot, we must accept that we are invoking a host of spiritual allies and energies—and the more aware we are of their personalities, the better able we will be to integrate their wisdom. Similarly for a practicing witch, we experience the world as animated, full of soul and spirits to connect and commune with. It is the role of the modern witch to be clear and confident about the historical and energetic frameworks of the tools we use to channel our magic.

The foundation of the tarot still emblazons itself onto imaginations all over the world to this day. I believe this strength comes from the power of symbols and the elemental relationship between symbols and humankind. Modern tarot practitioners have come to focus more on the inherent power of symbols. The study of symbolism can be a rich spiritual and psychological practice.

Symbolism operates on a different level than linguistics and reason. Receiving information through nonverbal or nonlinguistic methods and modalities changes the texture of the knowledge. Tarot is the paragon example of how we can use symbolism to integrate knowledge and wisdom in an intuitive or receptive way. Since the tarot is an assemblage of images, readers are asked to enter the "text" in a different way. As Swiss occultist Oswald Wirth explains,

"As soon as one is able to make the symbols speak, they surpass all speech in eloquence, for they allow one to find the 'Last Word,' that is to say the eternal living thought, of which they are the enigmatic expression." Each card has a message waiting to be conveyed to the inquirer who is ready to receive the message.

There is a sense that the symbols of the tarot allow one to understand every facet of our human potential. Whether we incline more toward the Devil archetype or the Lovers, we contain both tendencies within our psyches. In this way, tarot is also a tool for self-actualization. By placing ourselves in the context of each card, we are able to try on a new facet of being, with the hopes of achieving psychic wholeness. The tarot becomes the guide, the teacher, the map to self-actualization.

I believe that through the study of the tarot an aspirant will be able to feel their connection to the collective. A shift takes place when working personally with the tarot's symbols; pieces of the self are realized in each card. These aspects of self also represent the full range of human experience. Interpersonal connection to these ancient archetypes is as potent now as it was centuries ago. Tarot is not only a tool for self-actualization—it expresses a fundamental interconnectedness; through tarot we reconnect with our basic need to live in a meaningful universe. May we find hope in the glimpse of a shooting star, feel exalted by the rising of the full moon, and whisper thanks for the gift of a wild turkey feather. The tarot offers a key through its symbolism, a key to rediscovering our place in the interconnected web of life.

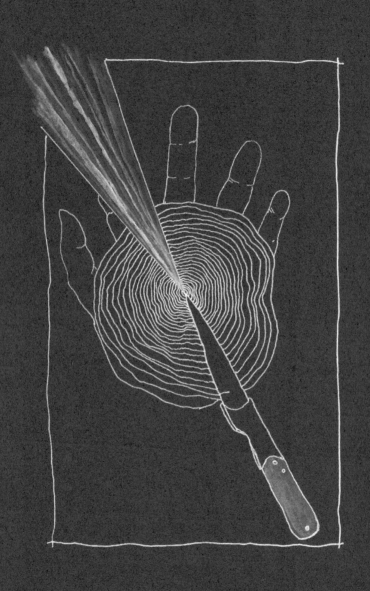

The Suits

The suits of the Wanderer's Tarot remind us of the immediate ways we can connect with the natural world, deepening our respect for the wheel of life and death. The suits of *Moons, Stones, Feathers,* and *Knives* were chosen out of the desire to improve our balance and harmony with the elemental world. When living in harmony with our environment, we are actively engaging with it. Likewise, to exist magically in the world is to be in direct communion with it.

We witches are energized by our stones, rocks, and crystals. We are elevated by our relationship with the moon. We are called upon by the flight of a bird, or the gift of a hawk's feather. We gather with our knives, and direct power with the blades.

MOONS

Moons correspond to the traditional tarot suit of Cups. They are associated with the element of Water. Just as the moon controls the tides of the ocean, the phases of the moon also illuminate our inner cycles. The moon affects our interior tides, guiding us through the ebbs and flows of our emotions. The suit of Moons speaks to our relationships with our emotional bodies, as well as how we react to the emotional well-being of others. The suit of Moons corresponds to the astrological signs of Cancer, Scorpio, and Pisces. The Moons rule the summer season, when the nights are warm and colored by her silver glow. The Moons also rule the heart center.

STONES

Stones correspond to the traditional tarot suit of Pentacles. Stones range from nonmetallic to crystalline, and are shaped by the movements and gestations of the Earth itself. The suit of Stones is associated with the Earth element for this reason, as well as carrying with it a grounding, nurturing force. Stones deal with material possessions and wealth, in addition to economy, and how we provide for ourselves. The suit of Stones is also associated with our health and our physical body. The ruler of autumn, Stones are related to the hearth, and how we tend to our homes. Stones correspond to the astrological signs of Taurus, Virgo, and Capricorn. The Stones rule our root systems.

FEATHERS

Feathers correspond to the traditional tarot suit of Wands. Finding feathers is widely accepted as a gift from the winged ones, and as an auspicious sign that some important message is soon to be delivered.

The suit of Feathers corresponds to the Fire element—specifically the fire that feeds our passions. Finding or collecting feathers is a reminder to stay tuned into our soul path, and to feed the parts of us that hold our true desires. The Feathers are a suit of action and creation. Ruling the spring season, Feathers remind us to reawaken and stoke our internal flame. The suit of Feathers corresponds to the astrological signs of Aries, Leo, and Sagittarius. The Feathers also rule the center of our will.

KNIVES

Knives correspond to the traditional tarot suit of Swords. Knives are an ancient tool, with an endless range of applications. At the beginning of time knives gave us the gift of cutting, separating, dividing, and gathering. The suit of Knives corresponds to the logical mind, and our intellectual faculties, as well as to the Air element. The main challenge of this suit is knowing when to employ our logical capacities and knowing when to listen to our intuition. Knives speak to the power of integrating the mind into powerful magical work. The witch's athame, or ritual blade, is used to direct energy and create magical boundaries. Ruler of the winter season, Knives are reflective and meditative in nature. The suit of Knives corresponds to the astrological signs of Gemini, Libra, and Aquarius. The Knives rule the mental plane.

The Court Cards

The court cards of *The Wanderer's Tarot* are nonhierarchical and not gender specific. The titles of Philosopher, Goddess, Prophet, and Wanderer aim to speak to the different phases of experience that a witch may journey through, while also corresponding to the traditional archetypes of Page, Queen, King, and Knight. When reading these particular cards, you may interpret them as people involved in your life, as representative of yourself, or as a lesson you may be experiencing.

THE PHILOSOPHER

The *Philosopher* questions all aspects of life. Fundamentally a skeptic, they like to turn over situations, emotions, and thoughts in their mind until they become polished stones, easy to swallow. Both student and teacher, the Philosopher teaches us about how we approach choice and challenge. They are consistently accepting and dismantling ideas. Romantic and serious, the Philosopher lives within us all. The Philosopher corresponds to the Page of traditional tarot decks.

THE GODDESS

The *Goddess* is an embodied character. They are strong and nurturing; knowing their positionality in the world, they emanate power. A symbol of flowering femininity, the Goddess likens to the mother archetype and has a compassionate aura. She teaches us how to feel like we are deserving, autonomous beings who have the power to create and change our realities. The Goddess corresponds to the Queen of traditional tarot decks.

THE PROPHET

The *Prophet* is in the esteemed position of soothsayer. They have prophetic tools and carry knowledge of how the future will unfold. With the heart of a seeker and the mind of a seer, the Prophet acts with intention and compassion. Because they are in such a powerful position, the Prophet's goal is to share their abundance with others, whether this be through advice or revelation. The Prophet's challenge is to fulfill their future predictions by the strength of their will and conviction. The Prophet corresponds to the King of traditional tarot decks.

THE WANDERER

The *Wanderer* is ready to take on the world, whatever it may throw their direction. A buoyant and stimulated traveler, the Wanderer feels most at home when they are in the process of getting lost. Their journey is fueled by their inward desire to "know thyself," as they have been the Philosopher, Goddess, and Prophet, and are ready to ascend to another level of understanding of their own being. The Wanderer is willing and ready to take on the cosmos, accepting all risk and reward that may come their way. The Wanderer corresponds to the Knight of traditional tarot decks.

A Note on Witches and Feminism:

Witch has many ancient associations and meanings. We are the wise ones, sharing our healing knowledge and developed psychic abilities. We are the spinsters, weaving the narrative of the empowered wild ones into reality. We are shapeshifters, bending consciousness to suit our will. We work in concert with the natural world, taking our cues from the intelligent cosmos, the wind, the wild spring, and the animals who cross our paths.

We are proudly reclaiming the responsibility of the witch. Past witches, the accused ones and those who practiced in secret, are our guides. By the light of the stars, our candles, and our sacred fires, we honor her, thanking her for her sacrifice and offering ourselves as vessels to continue the work. This is the work of showing up for our gifts. This is the work of healing ourselves, our mothers, our sisters, and Mother Earth herself. The work of the witch is the work of healing communities.

We are reclaiming Mother Earth as our spirit guide. By nurturing Earth, we are nurturing our bodies. The imbalances and destruction we are experiencing collectively reflects the mistrust and abuse of the sacred feminine; a sacred feminine that lives within each of us. The Wanderer's Tarot is an offering to the Goddexx. It is a way for us all to reconnect with their sacred wisdom, through the elements, our magical tools, and our own intuition.

We are reclaiming feminism as our fundamental code. By radically accepting our bodies, we accept all bodies. When we make peace with the sacred feminine, we learn to respect and treasure our given talents. By embracing feminism, we are inviting all beings to feel empowered.

As a feminist tarot deck, it asks all genders and spectrums to honor the Goddexx archetype.

THE FOOL

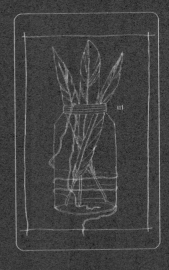

Spread Suggestions

First, *create space*. This space is for us to do our work. The space originates in our minds and is manifested through our surroundings. Light candles for Fire; offer a chalice of nectar for Water; keep your favorite gems and stones close, as an homage to the Earth; and allow for your songs, whispers, and chants to evoke Air.

Second, *set your intention*. In order to see a reflection clearly, the pool must be absolutely still, with no ripples. Your mind is the pool of the collective unconscious. It is the card's vessel to truth, and it is your choice to see with intuitive clarity. What truths are you willing to receive? What needs to be showered with divine light? What question needs to be answered?

Third, *mingle the cards of fate*. Shuffle the deck thoroughly three times. Cut the deck three ways. Have the seeker put the deck back together. Or shuffle the deck in whichever way you are drawn. Let life manifest in your palms.

COMPASS SPREAD

Position the cards in the four cardinal directions, and one in the center. Once the cards are drawn, notice how you feel pushed and pulled in different directions by certain cards, and which cards make you feel most at home. This spread is great to use as a general check-in, or when you are seeking new direction in your life.

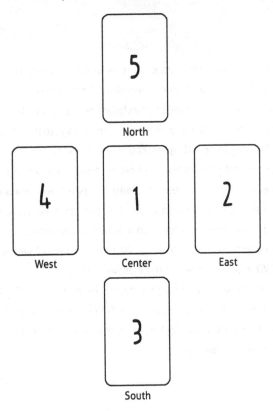

1. **CENTER—SPIRIT.** The central card represents your aura at this moment in time. It details how you are feeling, what has been influencing you, and how your energy is being perceived by others. This card will give us a snapshot of our spirit. The center card represents the fifth element: Ether. This is numinous energy that holds the web of life in balance.

2. **EAST—AIR.** As the sun rises in the east, this position signifies a beginning. Associated with Air, it is also the position of mental activity. How have you been exercising your intellect? Have you been communicating your visions, and sharing your voice with others? What thoughts have been cycling through your mind most voraciously? These are the questions solicited by this card.

3. **SOUTH—FIRE.** Return to your gut—back to the place of intuitive nature and innate drive. South is where you return to refuel and reconnect with your source. Associated with creativity, this position of the spread asks us how we are feeding our passions and stoking our imagination. Remember that inspiration is not always divine, and that fire needs oxygen and material to burn.

4. **WEST—WATER.** Where the sun disappears on the horizon, the west is often associated with the past. This position deals with all aspects of your emotional self. Think about your relationship to your emotions. Do you give them weight, or

disregard them as transitory? Consider the way you dream and use your intuition. This space can also speak to the relationships in your life.

5. NORTH—EARTH. The northern position speaks to the places and situations where we feel most at home. Also associated with our bodies, this space can deal with how we are balancing health and well-being. What is your connection to Mother Earth? Bringing up notions of how we create sacred space, this position of the spread shows us how to nurture ourselves and our larger communities.

PENTACLE SPREAD

The pentacle is an ancient magical symbol, imbued with incredible power. It has elemental associations that, when vibrating in harmony, symbolize a cosmic balance of external and internal well-being. This spread is fabulous for identifying blockages or imbalances in your energy fields. Each point of the pentacle relates to both an internal and external expression of self. Place the cards in the spread following the number guides, in the direction that you would draw a pentacle for protection and magical workings. Pay attention to how the cards you pull relate to their position on the pentacle. This spread is a great way to dive deeper into self-discovery and can often leave you with further questions.

The Iron and Pearl Pentacle practices are ways to psychically run energy between the points of the pentacle, which physically relate to points on your own body. I learned the Iron and Pearl Pentacle teachings from the Reclaiming Collective. The practice derives from Victor and Cora Anderson and their work with the Feri Tradition of Witchcraft.

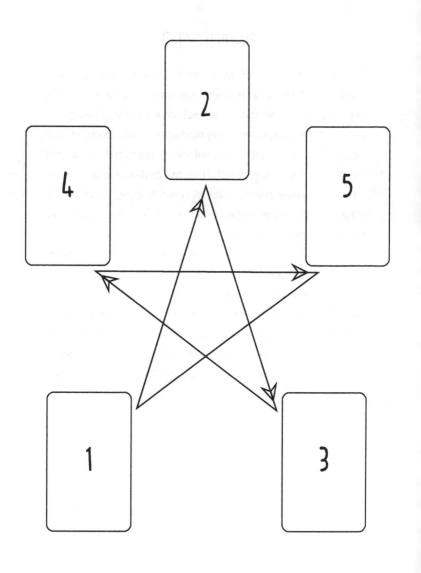

1.   **PRIDE + KNOWLEDGE.** This position of the pentacle asks, What is your magic and how do you share it with others? Consider the ways you relate to yourself with confidence. What is your knowledge and what are you seeking to know? Meditate on your sense of pride, as well as your relationship to knowledge.

2.   **SEX + LOVE.** This position of the pentacle asks you to identify your desires. How do you nurture them? What satisfies and excites you? What types of love are in your life? Meditate on your sense of sex: What does it mean to you? Meditate on how you accept love in your life.

3.   **PASSION + LAW.** This position of the spread seeks to expose what fuels your inner fire. What is it that motivates you to live life thoroughly, to traverse its valleys and its peaks? How does your passion influence your point of view? Meditate on self-imposed and societal boundaries existing in your life. What laws do you follow? Which do you break? What is it about your passion that negates or supports these systems?

4.   **POWER + WISDOM.** This position of the pentacle seeks to identify your relationship with power. What is your relationship to authority, and do you give yourself enough personal authority? Meditate on what you believe your wisdom is, if you feel you can identify it. What wisdom do you wish to carry? In what ways do you come to the aid of others by offering your wisdom?

5. **SELF + FREEDOM.** How do you know yourself, show up for yourself, and allow your truth to shine? This last position of the pentacle spread deals with the task of seeing ourselves with a compassionate and critical eye. In what areas of your life do you allow yourself the freedom to be wholly you? To be free is to be uninhibited, and it is to be in the service of your greater self.

BLESSING SPREAD

This blessing spread is a great practice for an everyday pull. It is essentially a way to illuminate your gratitude with the aid of a tarot card. By finding the blessing within the teaching of each Major and Minor Arcana, we are entering this tarot practice with the intention of a spell. Offering thanks is an extremely powerful way to connect with the Spirit.

1. **DRAW** a card that represents what you are thankful for.

2. **DRAW** a card to inform how to nourish and sustain such a blessing.

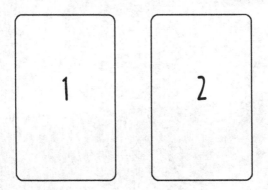

The Major Arcana

THE FOOL

Standing on a summit, surveying the mountains and calculating the distance to the horizon, the Fool steps toward a beginning. They are without many possessions, leaving their burdens behind. Only their wild nature, in the form of a dancing dog, is their companion on the journey ahead. The destination is unknown, but then again, isn't it always?

The Fool of the tarot is the numberless arcana, or 0, because it is the beginning of the journey. The 0 is a symbol for the cosmic egg, representative of an embryo waiting for fertilization. The Fool speaks to an abundance of potential energy. There are things to see and to experience. The Fool asks the seeker to invite the unknown into their life, in order for opportunities to arise organically.

REVERSED: The Fool begins their journey without a plan and with no concern for consequence. Perhaps more calculation is needed before you make your next step forward.

THE MAGICIAN

Finding her place of power, the Magician sets up her camp, honoring her magical allies. Yarrow and wild iris blanket the floor of the clearing she has chosen for her work. Painted on her forehead is an infinity symbol, as a reminder of cosmic abundance. Before her are the tools she uses with purpose and accuracy to direct her will.

The Magician card is a card of power and will. Laid before the Magician are her tools. These tools are unique to her experience, and she excels when she employs them. The teaching of the Magician is an affrmation and a reminder that you have what you need to work with in order to move forward on your path. There is a sense of dexterity inherent in the card that seems to say, "Go forth and do what you do best." Owning your skills, powers, and allies can be a long journey. If the Magician shows up in a reading, it is time for you to harness all that is completely yours.

REVERSED: If the Magician appears reversed in your reading, you are being asked if you know what your talents, skills, or tools are. If you do not know your strengths, you will not know how to play to them. It is time to learn more about your allies on the path.

THE HIGH PRIESTESS

Seated on her astral throne, the High Priestess has an aura of omnipotence. Commanding the flow of her magical consciousness with ease and awareness, she writes her history in a secret script known only to her and to her worthy adepts. She is the guardian of the veil between worlds and the source of occult inspiration. A representative for all virgin Goddesses, the High Priestess is the totally autonomous guardian of the sacred feminine.

The High Priestess is a powerfully feminine card. She exudes strength, knowledge, and independence, as well as a knack for psychic understanding. This card indicates expertise in a certain field, so own this knowledge! Others look to you for answers and understanding when they cannot find it for themselves. A very aqueous card, with strong associations to the moon and the element of Water, the High Priestess speaks to our receptive nature and asks us to turn within for answers. Pay close attention to your dreams and intuition when the High Priestess appears in a reading.

REVERSED: A reversed High Priestess can be calling on you to reconnect with your intuitive nature. The High Priestess lives within all of us, and she is an important aspect to nurture. Now is the time to recall dreams, sit quietly with yourself, access your creative side, and meditate. Perhaps there are certain repressed feelings that need to be addressed at this time, to avoid them manifesting negatively in your world.

THE EMPRESS

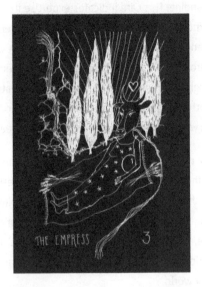

Waiting in an enchanted cypress grove, the Empress reclines on a blanket of stars. She is both Nuit and Demeter, mother of sky and earth. She is the ultimate creator, the pollinator of the natural world. The stream running through her grove originates with the High Priestess, and it is the stream of the unconscious. The Empress dips her toes into the water and creates dreams that manifest into realities.

The Empress is pregnant with the world and full of potential energy. An expression of divine motherhood, the Empress is a card of gestation and birth. What is it that you are harboring? What would you like to bring into the world? The original nurturing figure, the Empress calls for care and attention to detail. Be patient, and with focused expression your gifts will garner great appreciation. Remember to act with kindness in all dealings and to communicate with compassion.

REVERSED: Without good soil, your garden will not be able to take root and flourish. Pay close attention to how you nurture yourself, your ideas, and others in your life. Perhaps not enough care or kindness has been exercised, leading you to a less-than-ideal outcome. Be aware of how you treat the women in your world. They are all emanations of the Goddess, and the Goddess must be treated with respect.

THE EMPEROR

A ram's skull sits atop a carefully constructed cube, adorned with the symbols for Jupiter and Saturn. In the backdrop, jagged mountains loom, punctuated by two axes. The landscape is harsh and demanding, and the Emperor is exalted here in this land of strict discipline. The Emperor is the Ram, Mars, the one who implements and exacts plans with precision.

The Emperor symbolizes material order. A new business model, the outline of a novel, or the blueprints of a new home are all things relating to the Emperor's domain. With a shrewd eye and the willingness to dictate, they are totally focused on the implementation of structures, abstract or concrete. Whether the word structure makes you squirm or sigh, it is a key ingredient to successful follow-through in any endeavor. The Emperor can be an empowering guide when completing hard-to-accomplish tasks, or when you've been dragging your feet. When the Emperor card arises, it is wise to examine the structures you exist within. Which structures are beneficial to your success? Which structures are creating obstacles between you and achieving your goals?

REVERSED: Because of this emphasis on creating order, the Emperor archetype is also associated with patriarchy and systems that feel unbending or inauthentic. When the Emperor card is reversed, it may suggest that you practice too rigid of a routine, or have too authoritarian of an attitude. Be aware of how systems in your life can lead to more freedom rather than to cycles of oppression.

THE HIEROPHANT

She pulls aside the curtain that occults the mystery from our awareness, granting us entry into another realm, another world, or another way of understanding. The Hierophant is at once our guide and the key to unlocking further dimensions. Her mind is that of a beehive, constantly producing and facilitating the collection and storing of potent ideas that serve to nurture our souls.

Wisdom is the way of the Hierophant, for her truths are eternal. If the Hierophant has appeared, it is wise to stop pontificating and start listening. She is the revealer of secrets and is fundamentally a teacher, having experienced the unfolding and boundless nature of cosmic consciousness. Look to the people and resources in your life that carry wisdom. Now is the time to sit at their feet and listen to their stories. Focus on the intersection between your outer experiences and your inner knowledge. Allow your intuition to develop with the aid of a guide.

REVERSED: Are you eager to be told how to act, rather than finding the path on your own? When the Hierophant is reversed, it signals for you to start acting from your heart, rather than following the institutionalized pathways of society. Also, be wary of evangelists seeking to convert you to their way of thought. Remember that there are infinite truths, and your experience is just as valid as the next.

THE LOVERS

THE LOVERS

Drops of liquid love rain down from the astral plane of potential consciousness, presided over by the loyal Isis. The drops shower the prima materia *of the Earth and its devoted inhabitants. The Lovers below welcome the gift, accepting the love rain as their birthright. It flows through them, fueling their being with desire and passion.*

It is not easy to accept love into your life, but you cannot protect yourself from it either. Love is not always romantic; it is also platonic, devotional, and elemental to being. It is ubiquitous. Love is the act of being in harmony with divine consciousness. Once we allow our subconscious desires to align with our conscious desires, we love freely. If the Lovers emerge in a reading, begin or continue the process of opening your heart to the abundance of love in the world. Be open and ready to communicate deeply within your relationships and within yourself. The Lovers card symbolizes a union or bond, which may materialize in many ways. A successful union and partnership is built on fluid and free communication.

REVERSED: A reversed Lovers card is a sign of displaced or untempered love energy. Perhaps you are looking for validation and comfort in the wrong places. Maybe it is time to give more to yourself, rather than spending your energy trying to please others. Reorient your view of what love means, becoming more inclusive and less rigid.

THE CHARIOT

With the heart at the helm, this chariot is aiming for victory. The powerful and sensitive organ is bound and determined to stay on the path of its choosing. Graced by symbols of infinity and structure, the chariot is deemed noble by all who cross its path.

The Chariot is a symbol of success—success hard-won by following one's heart and personal convictions. Ruled by the heart chakra, its aim is to guide a seeker through any challenge with authenticity of being. If the Chariot is drawn in a reading, there is often a bright outcome on the horizon due to the diligence of the seeker. Use the Chariot to meditate on your desires and intentions, setting plans in place, and giving faith to your actions. The Chariot is not a card of chance; it is a card representing the cultivation of your will.

REVERSED: If the Chariot is reversed in your reading, you are being called to reconnect to your heart chakra. Perhaps your desires are misplaced, unrealistic, or not even yours to begin with. Now is not the time for action; it is the time to take internal inventory of what you truly want and how far you are willing to travel to get it.

STRENGTH

A fair maiden playfully massages the mouth of a handsome lion. The lion's mane is shrouded in a garland of wild flowers, matching the floral headdress of the woman. Through their physical connection they are linked, blurring the lines between human and animal. There is no fear or aggression apparent in either's spirit.

If the Strength card has been drawn, you are being asked to remember your personal creative power. Do not allow fear to cloud your path. Strength asks us to abandon our doubts, and remember that our realities are a mental creation. Notice how delicately the woman has her hands inside the lion's jaw. She is able to be so sure of her actions due to her connection to a storehouse of inner magical energy. Called kundalini by some, this coiled serpent of energy lies within us all, awaiting activation. Once activated, as it is within the spirit of the maiden, you are able to act courageously, without hesitations. Remember: you are the creator of your world.

REVERSED: A reversed Strength card can mean that your sense of self is out of whack. Are you allowing your resources to be sucked away by negative people and situations? Or are you spending your strength in places of inconsequence? In either case, do not let your fears rule your universe. Remember that you are strong, worthy, and divine. Feel into your body to regain connection to your personal rhythms.

THE HERMIT

Standing at the precipice, the Hermit leans in, inviting the void to draw closer. They are unafraid of the emptiness. With their palm outstretched, they send light into the darkness, heralding other seekers and lost ones to continue their search. Occulted by a candle, their features are inconsequential; their Truth shines forth to guide the way.

The Hermit occupies a space of solitude and reflection. They are the Recluse, Sage, or Wise Old One. The teachings of this card relate to the need for a time of inner journeying, or self-discovery.

It may also indicate the need for an alternative source of wisdom, perhaps from an institution or private guru. In either case, there is a thirst for knowledge that must be quenched in some way. You are in need of deep, ancient knowings to further your understanding of the nature of yourself, and of your time here in this incarnation. Time to journey out into the unknown, into the expanses of your inner cosmos.

REVERSED: When the Hermit is reversed, you are either being asked to resurface from the depths of your inner quest or you are being encouraged to spend more time solo, as a practice of self-care. The Hermit is wise, but tends toward loneliness. If the Hermit is reversed, it can indicate an imbalance in your social life and a need for deepening outward or inward connections.

WHEEL OF FORTUNE

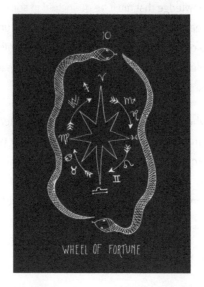

Two snakes form an Ouroboros around an eight-pointed star of Venus, orbited by the symbols of the zodiac. The central star is a symbol of the sacred feminine and the power of creation and fertility, while the astrological signs refer to our understanding of fate and how we converse with the cosmos. This space is ripe with opportunity.

"Let go, let go, let go, and expect good fortune!" will become your fresh mantra if the Wheel of Fortune has called on you. Illustrating the dynamics of our synchronistic and mythic universe, this arcanum serves as a reminder that some things happen for a reason. Whether you've been displaced or promoted, the Wheel of Fortune asks you to ignore rationalizations, and instead allow yourself to relinquish control. Sometimes it is important, and okay, to give the universe permission to move through you. The Wheel of Fortune signals a time to surrender.

REVERSED: A reversed Wheel of Fortune could suggest that you have been sacrificing control over your life due to external circumstances. Now is the time to fight back! While fate and karma play a role in each individual's path, it is not the sole ruler of our worlds. Feel empowered to act for yourself.

JUSTICE

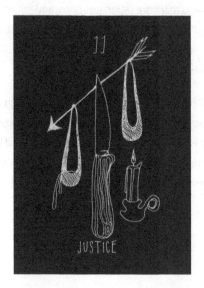

The scales of balance teeter on the point of a pocketknife. Air and water are weighed against one another, suggesting the need to make a choice executed with precision. The basket of water (symbolizing emotion) outweighs the basket of air (symbolizing intellect). A creative flame flickers beneath the air basket, fanning it upward toward the heavens.

Balance, equality, and fairness are all things associated with Justice. If Justice arrives in a reading, it is likely a good time to tune into your moral compass. If there are circumstances, individuals, or habits that are causing unneeded stress, Justice signals that it is time to seek a balanced path forward. It may symbolize weighty philosophical concerns that deserve plenty of consideration. Yet this is not a purely receptive card; Justice asks you to take action, definitively, in order to move forward on your path. If you are dealing with a confrontation of sorts, now is the time to make a decision. You will only know an outcome for certain once you have acted.

REVERSED: Injustice rules the world of a reversed Justice card. Injustice is directly related to an imbalance of the heart, whether that is a lack of respect or a biased thought. Time to reconnect to your heart center and reflect on the fairness that you hope to receive in your life. Delve deeply into questioning the root of your strife.

THE HANGED MAN

Tied to the limb of an old oak, the Hanged Man waits. Searching the water, they languish above, watching fish swimming upstream, and dreaming with the clouds' reflections upon the pooling waters. Suspended above the ebb and flow, they are able to think deeply.

In a state of total surrender, the Hanged Man is in a space of retreat and solitude. This is not a tortured state, but a state of meditation. In this special position, they are able to view their world freely. From this vantage point, the Hanged Man has a fundamentally different view of life, the world, and the universe. In this upside-down space, the ego's grip is loosened, accepting a higher mode of consciousness. The time to hold true to your path and your vision has arrived. Let the transition begin.

REVERSED: A reversed Hanged Man suffers from attachment issues. Whether you are attached to an idea about yourself or someone else, a place, a job, or a material reality, know that your ego is fooling no one. In a world based on flux, attachments are only burdens. Time to wake up to what is tying you down and make necessary adjustments.

DEATH

The skeletal grim reaper beckons to us, with a fresh-cut rose between their teeth and a sharp sickle at their feet. They are ready to dance. The sun is both setting and rising in this realm, over the Field of Endings, which they dutifully till.

Try not to fear the appearance of the Death card in a reading. The truth is that life is filled with a series of small deaths. A death could be the end of a job, the dissolution of a partnership, or a completely barren feeling that must be remedied. These small endings act like compost for your next life phase. Mourning is part of the grieving process and must be given time. Have faith that a new beginning is on the horizon. Listen to what your gut tells you when this card appears, and eliminate negative or stagnant energy from your life. It will refuel your will to live freely.

REVERSED: Are you hanging on to situations, people, or places that are feeding you negatively or in no way at all? Time to pull the trigger and rid yourself of these meaningless influences. Don't allow your insecurities and fears to hold you back from personal growth. If the sight of this card terrifies you, it is time to excavate your psyche and explore why you might have such a hard time letting go.

TEMPERANCE

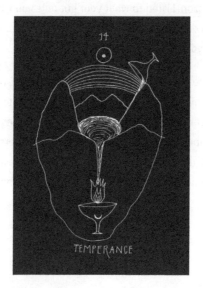

Luminous liquid slides from the chalice into a cool glacial lake, where it journeys into the next vessel, sublimating into flames. These changes in state are regulated and protected by the magi, who carefully controls the tempering behind the scenes.

The liquid of the Temperance card is consciousness itself. Imagine transforming cold, harsh, or negative thoughts into passion, creative inspiration, or pure love. This is the teaching of the Temperance card. Thoughts are potent vibrations that have the power to alter our physical energy. Know that you have mental control over your thoughts and you are not a slave to them. You are being continuously tested to find the right vibration by mentally juggling energy. Temperance reminds us to keep persisting in our efforts. While situations might arise that cause harm, all we can do is try to overcome. The work of transmutation is practiced.

REVERSED: A reversed Temperance card can suggest an imbalance in your mental and physical energies. Rather than allowing energy to properly flow through you, you're experiencing blockages, causing stagnation and unrest. Allow yourself the space to express freely. Identify what it is that you overindulge in mentally, and temper that emotion with its opposite. Mental alchemy!

THE DEVIL

THE DEVIL

Like an apparition in a dream, the face of the Devil surfaces. Their gaze is fierce, yet calm. With Mercury painted on their forehead, they come with a catalyzing message. Human hands outstretch to frame the key to the Devil's argument, the inverted pentacle.

The Devil is the ruler of the senses, perception, and sensuality. With often overpowering creative, sexual, chaotic energy, the Devil teaches us about our self-imposed chains, or "mind-forg'd manacles," as William Blake puts it. The Devil represents an awakening to the material desires that inform our every decision. Desires are erotic and pleasing, but they can be suffocating and may cause you to be driven purely by shortsightedness. Be aware of the ways in which you indulge. The first step toward spiritual unfoldment is acknowledging the flaws in your perception and actions stemming from illusion. The Devil is beckoning you to release yourself from your chains so that you might experience true personal freedom.

REVERSED: A reversed Devil signifies a position or mindset of extremes. Either you are overindulging in substances, sexual exploits, or your ego (most often the case), or you are a stubborn ascetic who suppresses most if not all of your outward senses. You might even be oscillating between these extremes, playing both sinner and saint. The Devil indicates that you are deeply trapped by your own experience. It is time to identify what is crushing you, and start the work of recovery.

THE TOWER

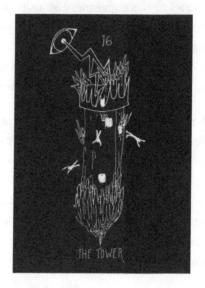

A great and unknowable force is directing an astral attack on your fortress. Lightning strikes when you least expect it. The fire catches quickly and consumes everything in its path. The only way to escape is to leap into the unknown.

The Tower is a card of major transformation. If life seems stagnant and you receive this card, be ready for significant movement. An event, mistake, or person is about to turn your world upside down. The lightning depicted on the Tower card is symbolic of a hard-hitting truth—one that you have been ignoring, or one that you desperately need to acknowledge in order to continue along your path. Be prepared to purge yourself of outdated and outgrown ideas. A new awareness, a new truth, and a new way of being are on the horizon—that is, if the lightning hasn't already struck.

REVERSED: If the Tower appears reversed, you may be clinging to a situation that is disastrous. If a house was on fire, would you stay inside? Time to gather your prized possessions and find a safe space to recover from your loss. Dramatic change is difficult to face, but it is often a necessary challenge on our journey.

THE STAR

The Star Goddess sits peacefully at the edge of a small pool. While she receives grace and nourishment from the soft starlight, she replenishes both earth and water with consciousness. The seven stars adorning her hair represent her twinkling chakra system, illuminated through her deep meditative work.

The Star offers a period of calm integration after a presumed period of unrest or upheaval. She encourages us to heal old wounds. Through meditation we are able to find inner equilibrium. This is the Star's teaching. She promises us reconciliation and peace by reminding us to stay hopeful. She can guide us through our inner planes to a place of true bliss, where we find our personal North Star that directs us on our path. Inherent in this process of renewal and rebirth is the need to give back. The Star encourages us to find our place in the cosmic cycle, the cycle of giving and receiving.

REVERSED: If the Star is reversed, you have found yourself in a place of deep darkness. Do not shun your talents and gifts. You are worthy, you are desired, and you are meant to be seen. Reconnect with that place of fundamental inspiration. Indulge in what makes you feel beautiful and perfectly you.

THE MOON

Feet firmly on the path, you are confronted by a still, dark well. The moon's reflection is silver and unmoving. Two dogs guard the path. One sleeps in fits of dreams while the other is enchanted, howling to the engorged moon. The pathway continues into the hills, and you can just see its outline in the silvery light.

The Moon is the card of the dreamer. If you indulge in psychedelic dreamscapes, escape to your inner world, and romanticize any circumstance, this card is exalted in your somnambulism. For those of us on the other side of the spectrum, you are being called to pay attention to your unconscious desires, activities, hopes, and fears. The unconscious realm is a deep and rich mine for self-discovery and creative content. Go there, and be prepared to learn a great deal about yourself and the other players in your world.

REVERSED: If the Moon is upturned, there are subconscious energies that need to be addressed at this time. Perhaps you have felt anxious, but you're unable to place the root of your anxiety. Depression and delusions are also facets of a reversed Moon card. Seek external guidance as to where you should be placing your truths. Do not be afraid of your deep Self.

THE SUN

Radiant and jubilant, the Sun is held gently in two giant hands. These are your hands, as the Sun is shining for you. Allow yourself to glow, to be nourished, and to exude warmth.

The Sun reminds us to simply be, in harmony with Earth's nourishing energies. She is the great life-giver on our planet, and without her we would be nothing. Offering a period of great happiness and a sense of purpose, the Sun card is truly a gift. Reflected in its astrological properties, the Sun rules over our character and ego. If the Sun is shining within your reading, the answer is yes and you should be elated to move forward, basking in the brilliance. The Sun may even signify some piece of lost knowledge that has come into clarity, giving way to an auspicious outcome.

REVERSED: Open yourself up to the possibility of happiness in your life. Regardless of past trauma or events, the reversed Sun is calling on you to allow yourself to feel the warmth of others, accept rays of sunshine with your heart, and reconnect with your inner child.

JUDGMENT

The all-seeing eye emanates and directs its life force down to the failing garden below. The saplings are in need of nourishment because the garden is transitioning from a state of cultivation to a wild glen. With divine aid they will succeed.

The Judgment card speaks to an intervention of sorts, heralding a transition from a materialistic view of the world to a spiritually holistic vision. It is about accepting and integrating a new viewpoint into being. This wake-up call is one of surrender. You are being asked to give way to what is outdated and realign yourself with the things in your life that truly feed you. If Judgment has appeared for you, it is time to take inventory of your karma, and open yourself up to your life's true calling. It is ready for you.

REVERSED: If Judgment appears reversed, you have been ignoring adventures, rebuffing cosmic calls, and just generally unwilling to wake up to the big picture. Time to loosen the chains that are keeping you from moving forward, and make a pact with yourself to accept the changes coming your way. Your life is calling, and your role in conscious evolution lies in the balance.

THE WORLD

She dances on the stars and skates through the nebulas of our galaxies. She is united, whole and pure consciousness. Protected by her guardians, she performs magical acts in harmony with divine flow.

As the final card of the Major Arcana, the World symbolizes a peak and a metamorphosis. It signifies the end of a period of struggles. Facing challenge, failure, and success, you have finally found your true rhythm. Your dance is in tune with Cosmic Consciousness. Each step is in harmony with your inward experiences and desires and is in concert with the Natural Law of life. The movements you are making are sustainable and holistic. Since you are now in the right place at the right time, you must continue to do your work, and see where the flow leads you.

REVERSED: If the World appears reversed, you have lost sight of your place in the larger cosmic narrative. Time to explore your karmic history to gain knowledge about how to successfully move forward to find your personal path. It may also signify a feeling of emptiness post completion of a major project.

TO WILL

TO KNOW

TO DARE

TO BE SILENT

The Minor Arcana

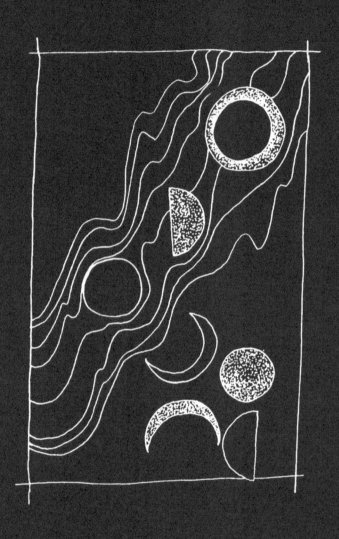

Moons

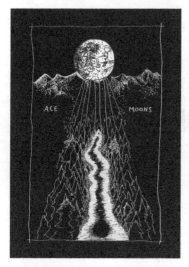

ACE OF MOONS

Conjuring up the depth one feels when following a moonbeam's reflection in the water, this card details a receptive place where we are open to healing and tuning into our psychic abilities. The water embodied by this moon is the water of our subconscious, brimming with intuitive knowledge of our true bliss. The Ace of Moons calls on us to discover our true beauty and our true divinity. It is a card that signifies a fulfillment of our spiritual quest.

REVERSED: A reversed Ace of Moons may signify that a spiritual understanding is on the way but is being delayed for some reason. Perhaps you are seeking consolation in illusory places with fraudulent guides. Perhaps you have been seduced by your subconscious, and it has led you to covet superficial beauty. It's time to contemplate the ways in which you define your spiritual life.

II OF MOONS

Suggesting union, the Two of Moons prepares one for a connection on an emotional level. Because love is chosen by the heart rather than the mind, the union has a subconscious attraction that must be observed. Seek partnership with your reflection, your opposite. In doing so, you may find balance in the desire for harmony. This card is a beneficial

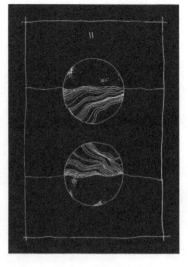

sign for those developing a soul-centered relationship. Now is a great time to indulge in romanticisms.

REVERSED: There may be a fundamental misunderstanding within a relationship at this time. A reversed Two of Moons can denote a severe imbalance in the energy being exchanged between partners or friends. Perhaps you are being called to shower yourself with love, rather than focus on others.

III OF MOONS

Rejoice! The Three of Moons has appeared to you as a sign that it is time to play. Typically a card that speaks to the need to celebrate, this card is infused with joy and bliss. The Three of Moons also speaks to the process of growth within a relationship. A relationship might be progressing to the next level, through the joint creation of your shared reality.

REVERSED: Beware of living your life solely by the principal of instant gratification. If the Three of Moons appears reversed, it can mean that you are overindulging at this time and are not taking your talents, or your emotions, seriously enough. This shallow existence can cause serious pain down the line.

IV OF MOONS

A love that does not evolve is condemned. The Four of Moons is a balanced card, yet it is one of stagnation. It is time to meditate on your relationships and how you work with their energies. It's also time to gain clarity on how you influence others, and also a time to cleanse yourself of negative thought patterns about your relationships. It is time to do some internal healing work.

REVERSED: If the Four of Moons is reversed, it is possibly time to start a new relationship, either with someone, with yourself, or with society. It is time to be social, and experience new points of view, for personal growth is on the horizon.

V OF MOONS

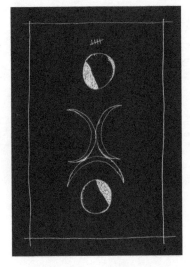

While two of the moons represented on the Five of Moons card are waning, the other three new moons suggest beginnings. The Five of Moons alludes to a time of great loss or emotional burden. Remember that is it important to grieve your losses and to experience catharsis. If something in your life is dragging you down, do not be afraid to cut the cord. If the Five of Moons has appeared to you, now is the time to say goodbye.

REVERSED: It is important to remember that loss creates space for new opportunities and new flowerings of energy. Seek comfort where you can successfully regenerate and slowly reopen your heart center.

VI OF MOONS

The Six of Moons represents a flowering of self-love. It has notes of nostalgia, and an overpowering emotionality. Elements from your past might be making a resurgence. This is a time for feeling all the feelings and could be a great time to channel your emotional energy into a creative outlet. The world is rosy through your eyes.

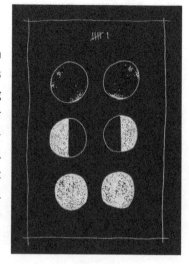

REVERSED: The opposite view of the Six of Moons can take on the form of self-indulgent, narcissistic love. The past is still very influential at this time, but it can become an escape, a place where you go to hide.

VII OF MOONS

When the Seven of Moons appears in a reading, it denotes an aura of confusion plaguing your life at the moment. Perhaps you have strayed from your true path or have been distracted by another's pursuits and have abandoned your own. In any case, you are unsure how to proceed and are being tempted by false ideals. Do not give in to the path that yields the most pleasure and takes the least amount of effort. It is time to exercise healthy self-control.

REVERSED: The Seven of Moons reversed is a good omen, which tells the seeker that they have successfully navigated a time of temptation or confusion, and are on the path to finding their true purpose. A deeper understanding of the simple pleasures in life awaits.

VIII OF MOONS

You are now being called on to negotiate a period of soul-searching. The Eight of Moons suggests that now is the time to hone in on a quiet spiritual practice. A dose of solitude now will sow many seeds of realization. There is a fullness in the moons depicted on this card that gives the message a sense of gravity. Find love in both heaven and earth, and all that is in between. The seeker must forgive her material pursuits, and seek a higher spiritual vibration.

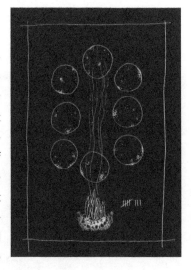

REVERSED: The Eight of Moons in a reversed position can suggest that a spiritual life has been ignored or abandoned for a more materialistic condition. It can also suggest that a traveler has been on the road, seeking for some time, and is ready to settle and create a home.

IX OF MOONS

The Nine of Moons suggests that it is time to sacrifice old habits that once helped the seeker but now serve to hinder emotional growth. A wishful card, the Nine of Moons signifies that the seeker is in search of more: more emotional stimulation or more range of feeling. In order for more to be provided, that which is holding you back must be assessed, and worn-out pathways must be left behind.

REVERSED: A Nine of Moons reversed may suggest that the seeker is overindulging themselves emotionally. Notes of vanity, greed, and self-pride are detected. Finding humility in your heart at this time will help you to keep your personal integrity intact.

X OF MOONS

Time to dance in the name of joy and love! The Ten of Moons suggests a time for communion with those who support you in the truest sense. Indicating a fullness of heart, there is great potential for sharing in the fullness of the present moment. This is a lighthearted card that suggests a bright future ahead.

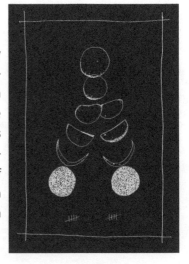

REVERSED: Sensitivity is key in dealings with loved ones. Exercise emotional caution, and remember to be grateful for the love in your life. Happiness is on the horizon, but there are a few obstacles on your path.

PHILOSOPHER OF MOONS

PHILOSOPHER OF MOONS

A philosopher is one who is constantly questioning, and constantly seeking the clear path. Carrying the badge of the Moon, she is constantly questioning her emotional positionality, whether it be within herself, in a certain situation, or in her relationship to society. The Philosopher of Moons is an idealist, a creative, and a dreamer.

Be prepared to offer yourself—and your full range of emotional potential—up to a situation in order to find a resolution. The philosopher undulates between the fear of getting hurt and the fear of not feeling her fullest. Allow your feelings to be known.

REVERSED: A time of emotional instability or haziness might overcome the seeker if the Philosopher of Moons is reversed. Check in with your expectations, and float a little closer to the earth. Try to find a safe place to feel grounded.

GODDESS OF MOONS

Fully embodied and emotionally ripe, the Goddess of Moons awaits the right partner, a glowing opportunity, or a kindred spirit. She is open and ready to be seduced by the moment. Her intuition is strong, and she is an excellent listener. She decodes the symbols of flowing water as if they were a narrative to be interpreted. The Goddess of Moons represents a proud and highly intuitive feminist. Be determined to not overthink situations, and instead act upon your emotions fearlessly.

REVERSED: The Goddess of Moons reversed can indicate an emotional manipulation by a close friend. Be aware of others' motives at this time, and be aware of your own motives. Strive to support others rather than oppress.

PROPHET OF MOONS

The Prophet of Moons carries with her an awareness of her own future. She understands the laws of cause and effect and can see how events could play out on the horizon. Open to these possibilities, she is stable and receptive. The garden flourishes around her and symbolizes a time blossoming with opportunity. While the Prophet receives insights, she gives back gratitude for her assumed position of clarity—this is what keeps her balanced. The Prophet of Moons has a giving, nurturing spirit. Practice this.

REVERSED: If the Prophet of Moons is reversed, the seeker is finding it difficult to make decisions for themselves. Do not be swayed by others' opinions or feelings. You are the ultimate guide on your path.

WANDERER OF MOONS

Guided by the ebbs and flows of the moon's cycle, the Wanderer of Moons is on a journey toward transcendence. Whether it be a spiritual quest or an emotional hurdle, the Wanderer is undergoing the process of spinning lead into gold. This is a gentle process, guided by the Wanderer's intuition and the knowledge that change is necessary in order to grow. The Wanderer has a strong sense of self and is also quite sensitive.

REVERSED: Perhaps the seeker is being too sensitive about a matter. Time to take a step back, and assume an objective eye if the Wanderer of Moons is reversed. This positioning may also indicate that the seeker is avoiding their own personal evolution and is not putting in the necessary work to move forward on their path.

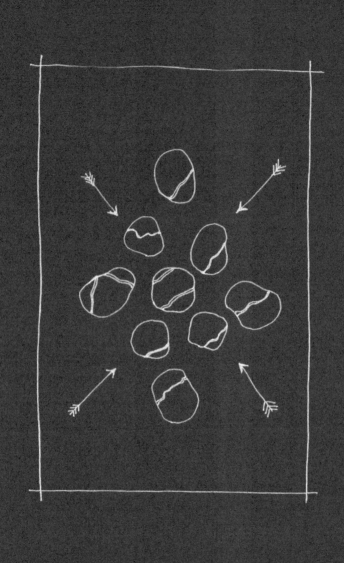

Stones

ACE OF STONES

ACE OF STONES

The Ace of Stones is a beginning. It asks for your intention as well as the potential energy needed to crystallize a new idea. The challenge is in the focus. Now is the time to be precise. Your energy will manifest into a physical project, a job opportunity, or, more generally, something that will sustain you materially as well as spiritually. Your ground is fertile, and success is blossoming around you.

REVERSED: Perhaps you have the intention to begin a new job or seek out a new shelter, but now is not the right time to act. More groundwork must be laid, and your intentions should be clarified before jumping into a new situation.

II OF STONES

Time for a dose of transformation! The Two of Stones is asking us to work with what we have to create a sense of abundance for ourselves. A reminder that energy is forever oscillating between potential and realized, you may be juggling more than one venture at this time. Do not feel overwhelmed; rather, be grateful for the opportunities that are presenting themselves to you at this time.

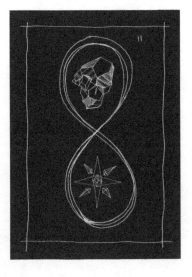

REVERSED: If the Two of Stones is reversed, the seeker may have taken on one too many projects. Decide what is currently most deserving of your influence based on the return it gives you.

III OF STONES

New energy has been brewing under the surface, and it is nearly fully formed. Whether it is a skill, an idea, or a new philosophy, it is time to prepare for a new chapter. Whatever has been gestating is ready to come forth and lead you to a new understanding and a new sense of stability. This is the beginning of your hero's journey, and you are about to uncover the path to your boon. This card suggests material validation for your steady work.

REVERSED: There is some recessed piece of knowledge that you have buried too deeply in your subconscious to access. What is it that you have abandoned in your life that could have been greatly appreciated by others? Do you feel there is something missing from your present, something you may have once known? Reconnect with your deepest desires, and you might find a fragment there that will aid in building your future.

IV OF STONES

The Four of Stones speaks to a time of incubation and inaction. Perhaps you are seeking to expand your influence, or increase your material well-being, but now is the time to go within, and return to a place of simple comforts. Why is it you feel you are in need of more? Take stock of your possessions and adopt a gratitude practice. Beware of being too cov-

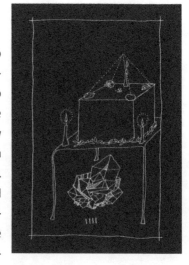

etous. Do not ruin yourself by buying into the myth of limitation. Remember, we live in a world of abundance, and it is our duty to share what we have an excess of.

REVERSED: The seeker is being too guarded and protective of their wealth. Because of this miserly attitude, they are on track to experience a great loss of liquidity.

V OF STONES

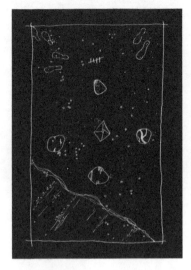

This is a time of transition in how you think about your income, your home, and economy in general. The Five of Stones suggests that the tides are changing. Do not hold too tightly to past assumptions of your well-being. You are now being asked to adapt and to have faith that a new dawn is on the horizon. Be conservative with your finances at this time.

REVERSED: This too shall pass. Although the Five of Stones reversed heralds a time of extreme caution in regards to finances, it also serves as a reminder that we alone can lead ourselves to redemption. There is much hard work to do, but there will be a new era of prosperity.

VI OF STONES

Celebrating both receptivity and action, the Six of Stones is a card of charity. In order to keep a strong financial balance, the seeker must realize that it is important to share wealth with those in need and to spend their money wisely. Purchase with intention. Support local businesses rather than greedy corporations. Be mindful of what you have and what you truly need.

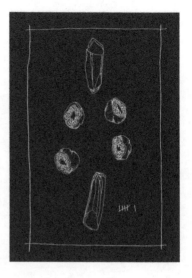

REVERSED: A reversed Six of Stones might suggest that you are in need of another's charitable acts. Do not feel ashamed to accept charity from others; rather, express authentic gratitude, knowing that if the roles were reversed you would do the same.

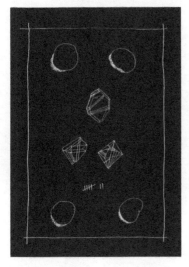

VII OF STONES

Congratulate yourself for being diligent and working with great intention toward achieving your goals. Now is the time to harvest what you have sown. Be aware that your hard work has paid off, and you are being asked to move forward to another phase of growth. Accept what is rightfully yours and be proud of your achievements.

REVERSED: Time to pay greater attention to your economic well-being. Your financial situation will not resolve itself without attention and effort on your part. You have either reached a plateau and are no longer gaining, or you have lost sight of your sense of stability. Take charge of your life!

VIII OF STONES

You have been working diligently toward your goals, constantly learning and improving your craft. The Eight of Stones acknowledges this effort, and asks you to continue on, despite a lack of external recognition. The energy surrounding this card is one of seeking perfection and asks for discipline. Dedicated to the pursuits of a passionate artist, the Eight of Stones serves as a reminder to continue to hone your passion.

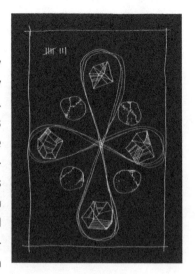

REVERSED: A reversed Eight of Stones suggests that there is more effort to be exercised. Do not become distracted and allow your skills and talents to go underutilized. Refocus, and reconnect with a project that might have been pushed out of sight. Your idle hands are in need of activity.

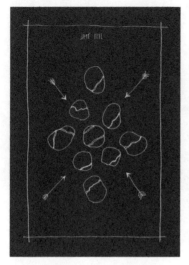

IX OF STONES

If the Nine of Stones has appeared, it is suggesting that you are enjoying the finer things in life. You have built an empire for yourself that allows you great comfort and enjoyment. Your wealth has exceeded that of others, and you alone can enjoy such riches. Remember to share what you have gained with others.

REVERSED: An upturned Nine of Stones suggests that you have sacrificed relationship and connection for your wealth and comfort. Now is the time to rebuild those relationships, and regress from a period of solitude.

X OF STONES

The Ten of Stones indicates that you have surrounded yourself with a family (however you define it) that supports one another. In this supportive environment there is great stability and wealth. This happy community will continue to serve you as long as you adopt a great understanding of the power of sharing. Under this auspicious influence you are better able to take risks and overcome challenges.

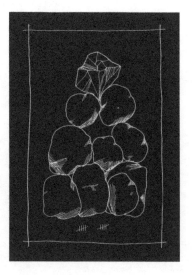

REVERSED: Perhaps you are entering a time of financial change, flux, or lack. If this is true, be sure to nurture your community, for they will aid you in your time of need. Another interpretation of a reversed Ten of Stones is a potentially financially secure community that is going through a period of unrest or disease. Time to re-evaluate what it is that makes you feel comforted and secure. Money is not the only factor.

PHILOSOPHER OF STONES

How do you spend your wealth? How do you save it, and why? The Philosopher of Stones deals with these questions. Perhaps now is the time to review your financial situation, or pay closer attention to how you define your sense of economy. The Philosopher is also a figure that denotes education and study. The card may indicate the need for schooling in order to further a career.

REVERSED: A reversed Philosopher of Stones suggests that too much attention is being paid to luxury items. Time to reassess the ways you are spending your money, and give your wealth to those in need.

GODDESS OF STONES

In reverence and strength, the Goddess of Stones appears to remind us to be grateful for our riches and what we have accomplished for ourselves. You are either in a very stable position in your life or have a welcomed benefactor who is. In either case, it is wise to take stock of your possessions and take note of how you arose to this place of power. The teaching of Stones is also about quietude; best not to boast or brag about your success but to feel great internal pride.

REVERSED: What was once yours may fall into another's hands if you do not protect it. Be sure to act with intention in all exchanges of wealth and energy. In particular, work on supporting your immune system at this time.

PROPHET OF STONES

Seek guidance for yourself and others through your own means and methods. The Prophet of Stones symbolizes an individual who is fully aware of their personal power to assess a current situation and move forward with wisdom. There may be many questions relating to stability, shelter, or economy at this time. Have faith that with time and consideration, you will be able to discern the right way forward, through, or back.

REVERSED: While you are able to divine your own way, you are so overwhelmed with the messages that you are unable to listen to your guides. Clear your mind of all your preconceived notions about how your life is supposed to be, and accept your circumstances and opportunities as they arrive.

WANDERER OF STONES

WANDERER OF STONES

Accepting your place in the flow of nature is a difficult task, but you are being asked to let go and travel on the winds of fate. You may not be in a place to begin a project, start a business, or buy a house, but you are being asked to journey and discover. The Wanderer of Stones reminds us that good things come to those who are open to such gifts. Give yourself the chance to experience life unfettered.

REVERSED: It seems that a period of travel and loose ends is drawing to a close. Perhaps it is time to regain your sense of place and purpose, and allow some roots to grow. Remember that you will wander freely again.

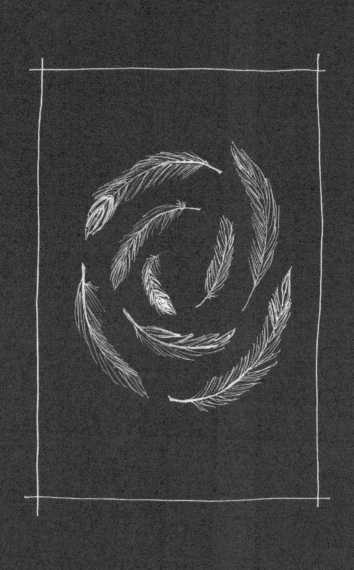

Feathers

ACE OF FEATHERS

A dwindling candle warms a nest of feathers, coaxing the egg to hatch. Symbolic of a birth process, the Ace of Feathers heralds a new beginning, whether it be a partnership, enterprise, or newfound passion. Be prepared to start following the thread of your desires to fruition.

REVERSED: You are eager to begin a new chapter, but a reversed Ace of Feathers suggests that conditions are not right at this time. Pay attention to where and how you are spending your time, and be sure you are creating space for your passions to flourish.

II OF FEATHERS

Two peacock feathers point in opposite directions, suggesting choice and the desire for balance. The Two of Feathers suggests an abundance of resources, and a confusion as to how to put them to use. Know that you have what you need to continue your creative journey. Work toward balancing your existence with a spiritual practice.

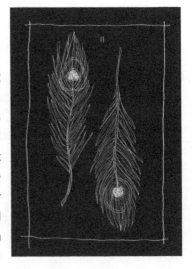

REVERSED: If the Two of Feathers appears reversed, you are in store for a surprise. Whether it comes in the form of a cameo from an old friend, an anonymous gift, or a mystical vision, your situation is about to be infused with excitement. Let it feed your creative fire!

III OF FEATHERS

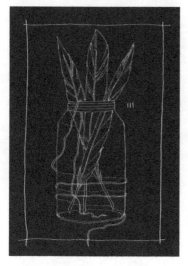

Three cozy feathers nestle against one another in their place of reverence. Their intimacy is natural and their magic is effortless. The Three of Feathers suggests that you are moving toward your goals with ease, possibly with the help of collaborators. Continue to follow the thread of your inquiry, for there are many possibilities on the horizon.

REVERSED: The Three of Feathers reversed signifies a blockage in your creative flow. You are having trouble communicating, or following through, and you are generally feeling disconnected from your inner fire. Breathe out your anxiety, and take baby steps toward completion.

IV OF FEATHERS

A card of retreat and rejuvenation, the Four of Feathers asks us to return home to recover. It is easy to get burned out when we are continuously asked to show up and give our energy to others. Be cognizant of your energy levels. Refuel with sleep, meditation, nutritious foods, and joyful activities. Your creative work will thank you for it later.

REVERSED: If the Four of Feathers is reversed, you are being asked to step out of hiding and resume your work. It's time to begin, complete, or continue serving your creative self. Share your skills and talents with your community.

V OF FEATHERS

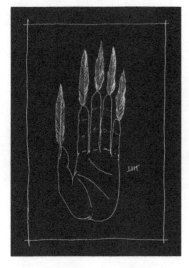

Five feathers have sprouted from the fingertips of your hand. You are being asked to consider the ways in which you collaborate with others and how you are able to integrate different ideas to find a place of harmony. This card can denote a type of struggle to find dexterity. Know that you were given all the tools; it's all about knowing how to put them to use.

REVERSED: Do not be afraid to share your unique opinion in a group or community space. All voices must be heard, even if they are in opposition to others' point of view. Be careful to communicate from a peaceful place, rather than from a place of fear or resentment.

VI OF FEATHERS

A garland of wild turkey feathers is strung together and presented to you as a reminder of your accomplishments. You have found yourself in a leadership position due to your authenticity and courage. Remember to practice gratitude for your gains, and be aware of the needs of others in your circle.

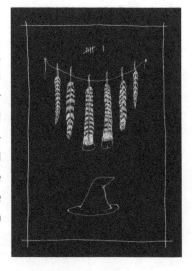

REVERSED: Your presumed success is built on arrogance and greed. Notice the tactics you have used in the past to get what you want. Victory gained through manipulation will only come back to haunt you.

VII OF FEATHERS

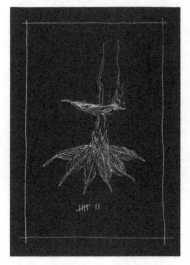

A sacred fire burns a pile of feathers, as one raises from the flames and turns to ash. There is an element of your life that is holding you back from creative fulfillment. Whether it is a habit, a negative thought pattern, or a person, sacrifice is needed in order to continue moving forward on your path.

REVERSED: You are experiencing great blockages in your energy at this time. A reversed Seven of Feathers suggests that you are either being too protective or you are allowing people and situations to rule you. Take control of your path, stand your ground, and step into the flow. Ultimately you know what you need in order to grow.

VIII OF FEATHERS

Whimsically swirling inward and outward, the Eight of Feathers suggests the cultivation of order in your life. You are being asked to dissolve some aspects of your life, and integrate others into your being. This card may symbolize the need for a meditative activity in your life. Create pathways and habits that are nourishing for mind, body, and soul.

REVERSED: Perhaps you have become stuck in a negative cycle or pattern, and haven't been able to reorder your world. Take apart the elements of the cycle so that they no longer work in concert. Be clear about your intention to change.

IX OF FEATHERS

A well-worn witch's hat is stuffed playfully and proudly with a collection of feathers. The Nine of Feathers suggest that a period of great work and effort is nearing the end. Take some time now to count your victories, and see your accomplishments with humility and gratitude. You may have already met or will soon meet a spirit guide who has been aiding you along your path.

REVERSED: A reversed Nine of Feathers may suggest that you have reached a dead end. It is easy to become stuck in our ways. It's time to change up your process, rewrite the poem, or start a new painting altogether.

X OF FEATHERS

What was birthed with the Ace of Feathers finds fruition in the Ten of Feathers. Your artistry has flowered, projects have launched, and your community is participating and interacting with your work. Be aware of your newfound responsibility and sense of self. Grow into your new set of wings.

REVERSED: If the Ten of Feathers is reversed, you are realizing that you have taken on more than you can shoulder yourself. It's time to ask for assistance with your work, reassess your commitments, and be prepared to challenge yourself further.

PHILOSOPHER OF FEATHERS

With one foot hovering over the ledge and the other floating over the rabbit's hole, the Philosopher of Feathers has pledged to follow their passions. Whether they will move forward, through, or fly above is the next concern. The Philosopher is intent on the quest of self-discovery. A free spirit with their creativity ruling their world, they are deep in the cosmic space, constantly negotiating a form of actualization. Rather than calculating which road will be the most fulfilling, grow into your wings and leap.

REVERSED: A reversed Philosopher of Feathers suggests that your freewheeling nature has led you to experiences that are wild and overwhelming. Due to the fact that you are not integrating your experiences, you are left feeling empty and unfulfilled. The energy of a reversed Philosopher of Feathers is hasty, someone who acts out of ignorance rather than from a place of enchantment. Reassess or reclaim your motives. Act with the intention of self-actualization, rather than seeking a good high.

GODDESS OF FEATHERS

With wings outstretched, the Goddess of Feathers is effused in a flurry of down. Her wings are molting, constantly accommodating new growth. She is motivated by her passions and is fed by her creative outlook on life. Because of this, her actions are truly authentic and she radiates joy for life. In a position of compassion and privilege, the Goddess is able to help others find confidence and success along their path.

REVERSED: If the Goddess of Feathers is reversed, she has an aura of jealousy and deceit. Something is hindering your personal growth—whether it be your own negative thoughts or a negative being in your life. Be aware of who and what challenges you. Surround yourself with positivity and those who support your dreams with no strings attached. An encouraging challenger may be a good friend to you at this time as you work through these psychic and physical blockages.

PROPHET OF FEATHERS

Unafraid to flaunt their courage, beauty, and creativity, the Prophet of Feathers lounges on a magnificent bed of peacock feathers. Having acted from a space of originality, they are perfectly proud of their accomplishments. In a place of esteem, the Prophet has gained new knowledge and integrated old ideas. Experiencing a creative peak, the Prophet knows their good fortune and is willing and able to give advice to other seekers who are also on the path.

REVERSED: A reversed Prophet of Feathers suggests an air of arrogance and secrecy. Rather than being forthcoming and sharing their prosperity with the community, the Prophet will hide away, coveting their beauty and assets to their own detriment. All of their hard-earned confidence will vanish once there is no one to seek ego validation from. Sharing your creative genius is part of experiencing success.

WANDERER OF FEATHERS

Standing in a fluid meditation pose, the Wanderer of Feathers surrounds themselves with and indulges in beauty. Driven by their desires and their passionate nature, the Wanderer seeks new forms of experiencing consciousness with body, mind, and spirit. Allowing themselves to flow freely, the Wanderer is able to find creative solutions to dilemmas without stress or anxiety. The teaching of the Wanderer of Feathers is to follow your passions wherever they may lead—first and foremost with an open mind and a clear sense of self.

REVERSED: A reversed Wanderer of Feathers may be suffering from an overblown ego that likes to take them on nefarious trips into and through other people's lives or realities. Without a cause or motive, the Wanderer's misplaced energy is left to take gambles and make risky moves, leaving a wake of heartbreak behind them. There might also be travel hindrances associated with a reversed Wanderer of Feathers. Before you decide to follow your passions, make sure they are directly serving your personal growth, rather than fulfilling a shortsighted whim.

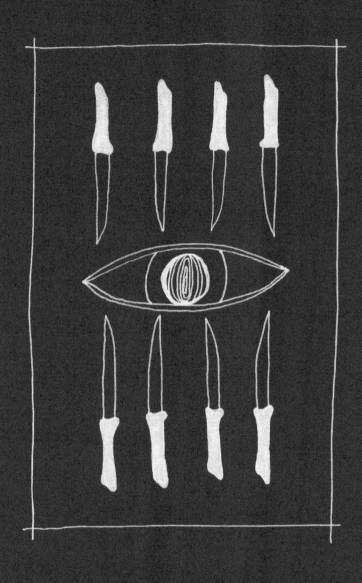

Knives

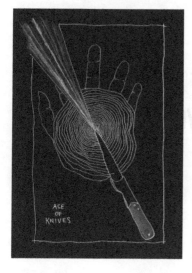

ACE OF KNIVES

The knife strikes its target in the center of the open palm. This signifies the beginning of a new creation. This could manifest as a new business model, the idea for a movie script, or a new understanding about the self. In any case, the seeds of a thought have been planted, and the mind knows how to nourish the thought into fruition through the power of will.

REVERSED: You may be experiencing a period of mental stagnation. Having been creative and mentally active in the past, you are now in a mental lull. Don't stress about this feeling of lack; rather, reconnect to mental activities that have given you great pleasure in the past.

II OF KNIVES

The Two of Knives suggests a moment of choice: one knife is pointing into a chalice, receptive, while the other knife seems ready to act, alert. You are weighing your options carefully by exploring both outcomes, but this is not the moment to act or choose. Hold space for both perspectives and strive for equilibrium.

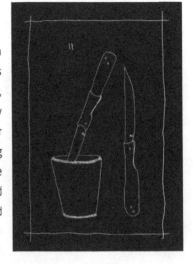

REVERSED: You can no longer sustain a stalemate and must take action. Whether the outcome you choose is "right" or "wrong," a piece of truth will be revealed to you.

III OF KNIVES

Collecting berries can be an act of sweetness, or it can leave you studded with thorns. What seems to be an innocent activity turns into a painful memory. The Three of Knives suggests heartbreak due to an incongruity. Perhaps your love, or your lover's intentions, weren't genuine. In either case, the time has come to face the facts. Conflict is inevitable.

REVERSED: Now is the time to grieve, feel deeply into your sorrow, and hopefully begin to heal. This process is thorny and takes time, so be gentle with yourself. During these times of tenderness, be sure to keep yourself psychically protected.

IV OF KNIVES

If the Four of Knives appears in a reading, it is time to retreat and recover from some sort of mental exertion. You have depleted your mental storehouses, and it is time to regenerate. Activities related to sleeping and dreaming will be helpful to you now. Focus your energies inward to recover your sense of intellectual power.

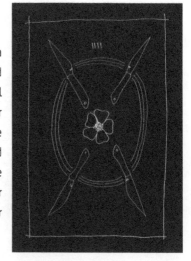

REVERSED: You might feel as if you are awakening from a prolonged dream or perpetual haze. Clarity awaits you once you regain awareness and your sense of self.

V OF KNIVES

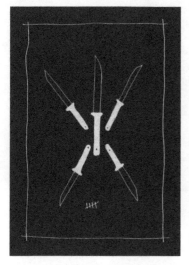

All five knives are pointing in different directions. Your mental faculties are thrumming, actively pursuing an idea, cause, or argument. However, rather than working in concert, your mind is scattered and spreading itself too thin. Time to collect these disparate pieces and realign with your purpose.

REVERSED: You may be weighed down with overwhelming feelings of remorse. Due to your inability to act intentionally, you have caused more damage than good. Look for fragments of the situation that you can salvage and turn into silver linings.

VI OF KNIVES

The time has come to take a mental or physical journey in order to gain perspective on a subject that has been causing you strife. Try to objectively examine your situation through meditation. Use your discerning eye to fashion new judgments. Remember that the suit of Knives relates to Air, as it reminds you to inject levity and movement into your logos.

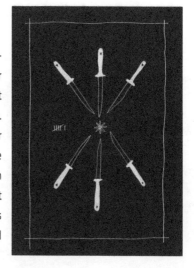

REVERSED: Don't become stuck in your mental state. You are in desperate need of a change of pace. Look inward, and prepare to engage in deep soul-searching in order to reorient your mind.

VII OF KNIVES

Circumambulating an idea and narrowing your focus are the main objectives of the Seven of Knives. Hone in on what it is that you are trying to communicate, plan, or execute. Seek to integrate all the elements involved and find a place of objectivity moving forward.

REVERSED: With so many irons in the fire, you are unable to decide how to proceed with a task, project, or trajectory. Be wary of becoming so distracted by the task at hand that you lose your sense of self-care.

VIII OF KNIVES

The eye in the center of the Eight of Knives represents our critical nature. You are being asked to bring care and attention to your actions. You are enwrapped in your own judgments, and the judgments of others, and this may be constricting your process. To alleviate this anxiety, pay attention to this card's reversal teaching.

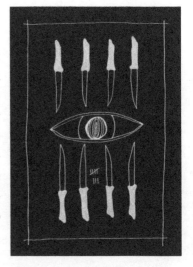

REVERSED: You are in a position of higher attunement and learning. By finding a place of objectivity through meditation, you are able to understand the situation in a different light. Practicing mindfulness will continue to be beneficial for you along the path.

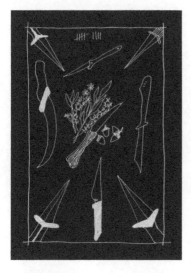

IX OF KNIVES

Here Knives are scattered in a seemingly random pattern, yet are actively engaged in the activity of harvest. The Nine of Knives speaks to how we collaborate within our community. What skills do we bring to the table, and are we actively listening to others? This card signals conflict and the neglecting of others' contributions.

REVERSED: You have narrowly escaped a major fallout with a community of like-minded individuals. Or perhaps you have been surrounded by people who are ignoring your contributions. In either case, know what skills you have to share, and be prepared to share them in order to persevere.

X OF KNIVES

Signaling the conclusion of a period of immense mental activity, the Ten of Knives is a card of completion. Framed by wild roses and lilies, this card suggests a flowering of being. Relish in your accomplishments! Having discovered a sense of balance, you are now able to engage in both receptive and active mental activity. You may rest here, and reflect on

your success before continuing on with your work.

REVERSED: When the sharp edges are all pointed at you, you can be sure you are not safe. Perhaps you are anxious about the future and are unsure how to finish something you started. Be careful not to rush too quickly into closing this chapter of your life. There may be unfinished business that you need to deal with before you can move on.

PHILOSOPHER OF KNIVES

With arms and legs made of pocketknives, the Philosopher of Knives is eager to exercise their knowledge in any way possible, at any given moment. The Philosopher represents a student, or someone in the process of learning a great deal. They are excited and ready to engage. With one foot in the fields and one foot in the stream, they are exploring a wide range of territory and discovering where they feel most intellectually at home.

REVERSED: Incapable of making a decisive claim or choosing a single pathway, the Philosopher of Knives is trapped in the realm of possibility. Having learned a great deal, the task of integration is at hand; now is the time to practically apply learned knowledge. The challenge of the reversed Philosopher of Knives is to commit to an ideal.

GODDESS
OF KNIVES

Steadily at work in the fields, the Goddess of Knives harvests what will sustain her through the upcoming winter. She exudes stability while her third eye is buzzing, activated. Representing transcendental consciousness, the Goddess knows the power of her intellect and also realizes its limitations. Seeking balance, she mirrors her

mental activity with bodily expression. Experience and define the relationship between your own body and mind. Be sure that one is not outworking the other.

REVERSED: If the Goddess of Knives is reversed, you would be wise to consider how you communicate with others and how you share your intellect with the world. Perhaps you have become too physically or spiritually isolated and are in need of a teacher, stellar novel, or piece of ecstatic music to boost your mental drive. Seek intellectual stimulation.

PROPHET OF KNIVES

Standing spread eagle, the Prophet of Knives creates a physical temple of themselves, complete with offerings of gratitude. With their keen and critical nature, the Prophet works diligently and with the discernment of a judge. They retain an innate knowing of how to clarify, communicate, and edit their world in order to make clear their case. The Prophet signals a time to rework an old mental pathway, or try a new methodology on an old set of problems. New thought patterns are on the horizon.

REVERSED: In a reversed position, the Prophet of Knives takes on the role of a stern disciplinarian. They are cold and unbending, which can be poisonous for innovation. Allow yourself more mental freedom. Explore rather than investigate. Do not forget to act with humility, and remember, you don't know everything.

WANDERER OF KNIVES

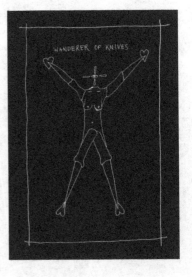

The Wanderer of Knives speaks to an intellectual seeker, someone who collects ideas and weighs them skeptically, while allowing themselves to indulge in utopian fantasies and idealized outcomes. The Wanderer works with courage to integrate mind and spirit, so that their mental activities are heartfelt and compassionate. If the Wanderer of Knives appears in a reading, it is wise to evaluate your relationship to learning. Maybe it is time to take an intellectual leap of faith, or go on an educational adventure.

REVERSED: A reversed Wanderer of Knives suggests you have lost a sense of true knowledge. Maybe you continue to circle around ideas without getting to their heart, or you are an intellectual butterfly, never fully finishing a task. Now you are being challenged to go deeper into your work and understanding, to fully commit with your heart as your guide.

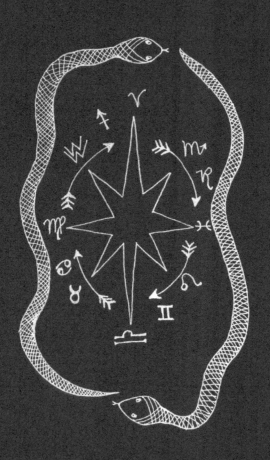

ARTIST STATEMENT

The tarot has been a source of Truth in my life for the majority of my years. It is my way of attuning to the collective, understanding my boundaries, and how I keep step with the cosmic dance. My tarot practice has illuminated how I intersect with the web of all existence, as well as the many facets of my own personality. The cards have shown me the true nature of synchronicity, and how we are all cocreating reality simultaneously.

The birth of the Wanderer's Tarot was driven by the desire to create a tarot deck that honors the feminine, as a power to embody, and as a challenge to embrace such strength. Created within a ritualistic framework, the deck holds true to the process of magic, and encourages others to engage in manifesting self-knowledge. For the seekers who cannot sit still, and for the journey's moments of reflection, the Wanderer's Tarot speaks to the wilds of the heart and mind.

As an artist I wander through mediums and modes of creation, always in relationship to Spirit. To all of you out there who are spiraling with the magic—keep spinning, and never be afraid to share your love of the craft with others.

ABOUT THE AUTHOR

At home in the overlooked intersections of dreams, meadows, and used bookshops, Casey has always known herself as a witch, hedge-walker, and weaver between worlds. Having been gifted her first tarot deck for her thirteenth birthday, Casey began her occult and magical studies early on, and her fixation with enchantment has been a strong thread through her life and work ever since. Her published divinatory tools include *Wanderer's Tarot* and *Wyrd Sisters* oracle. In 2018 Casey founded Modern Witches and hosted her first Modern Witches Confluence—a symposium for seekers and witches featuring presentations from Aja Daashuur, Mary Grisey, and Starhawk over Samhain weekend. Modern Witches continues to host educational spiritual gatherings, and Casey hosts the *Modern Witches Podcast*. Casey's life and work aim to uplift the healing power of witchcraft, particularly as we face unprecedented planetary crises. Currently living in Mount Shasta, California, Casey can be found wandering through the forests, baking bread, offering oracular counsel, and making art in collaboration with her spirit helpers.

To Our Readers

Weiser Books, an imprint of Red Wheel/Weiser, publishes books across the entire spectrum of occult, esoteric, speculative, and New Age subjects. Our mission is to publish quality books that will make a difference in people's lives without advocating any one particular path or field of study. We value the integrity, originality, and depth of knowledge of our authors.

Our readers are our most important resource, and we appreciate your input, suggestions, and ideas about what you would like to see published.

Visit our website at *www.redwheelweiser.com* where you can learn about our upcoming books and free downloads, and also find links to sign up for our newsletter and exclusive offers.

You can also contact us at *info@rwwbooks.com* or at

Red Wheel/Weiser, LLC
65 Parker Street, Suite 7
Newburyport, MA 01950